WELLNESS WHYS: DECODING THE 50 CAUSES OF ILLNESS

2

Contents

Introduction:

Thank you for visiting "Wellness Whys: Translating the 50 Reasons for Ailment." We embark on a journey to unravel the complexities of human health and investigate the myriad factors that contribute to illness in this comprehensive guidebook. The first step toward creating a life of vitality and well-being is to comprehend the factors that make us susceptible to various health issues.

As we dig into every section, you will acquire experiences into hereditary inclinations, way of life decisions, ecological impacts, and a plenty of different components that assume critical parts in forming our wellbeing predeterminations. "Health Whys" isn't simply a gathering of purposes behind sickness; It is your road map to empowerment, providing you with the information you need to make educated health decisions and take preventative measures.

Go along with us on this edifying investigation, where we demystify the intricacies of the human body and psyche, offering you a comprehensive point of view on health. Together, we should explore the different scene of wellbeing, outfitted with the comprehension that will enable you to have an existence of imperativeness and strength. Let's unravel the reasons behind wellness and pave the way to a happier, healthier you right now to begin the journey.

1.1 Outline of Sickness

It is fundamental to lay out a key comprehension of what sickness really involves before we continue on toward the unpredictable trap of elements that add to disease. In this part, we'll explore the various kinds of disorders that impact human prosperity. We'll show the various challenges our bodies can face, from stressful situations to ongoing illnesses. An inside and out examination concerning the basic reasons for illnesses starts with a comprehension of their range.

1.2 Meaning of Getting a handle on Causes

Why might it be really smart for us to pass on a journey to decipher the purposes behind sickness? In this portion, we unravel the significance of getting a handle on the secret factors that influence our prosperity. Diving into the purposes behind infection empowers individuals to proactively take care of their thriving. Countermeasures, early identification, and informed navigation all benefit greatly from having knowledge of these causes. Oblige us as we examine the phenomenal impact that understanding the explanations behind disease can have on private and total prosperity results.

2. Innate Factors

2.1 Obtained Conditions

Set out on an innate trip as we research the impact of gained conditions on our prosperity. Look at how certain circumstances are gone down through ages and impact our vulnerability to sickness to study the multifaceted idea of hereditary legacy. We'll investigate the spaces of natural sicknesses, uncovering understanding into both the known and the potential genetic markers that expect a section in framing our prosperity destinies.

2.2 Genetic Tendencies

Not all clinical issue are destined, yet many have an innate part that can increase weakness. In this portion, we'll break down the possibility of genetic tendencies — understanding how our innate beauty care products can make a tendency to explicit sicknesses. Oblige us as we unravel the delicate agreement among genetic characteristics and lifestyle choices, laying out the basis for informed prosperity decisions.

3. Way of life Choices

3.1 Food and Diet As indicated by the saying, "The kind of food you eat will impact you general prosperity," Examine the huge impact of diet and food on your prosperity. We'll take a gander at the a wide range of parts of food, from supplements that fuel your body to the typical snares of unfortunate dietary patterns. Figure out what your dietary models mean for your flourishing and how to keep a sound eating schedule that is both changed and filling.

3.2 Unique work

Move past the decent way of life as we jump into the basic control of dynamic work in pushing flourishing. Track down the potential gains of standard movement, including mental and cardiovascular prosperity. Whether you're a seasoned wellness enthusiast or just starting out, this section provides advice on the best way to incorporate active work into your daily routine.

3.3 Substance Abuse

Our choices concerning substance use can essentially influence our prosperity. Uncover the staggering association between substance abuse and different clinical issues. From the effects of alcohol and tobacco to the repercussions of unlawful prescription use, we'll explore the diverse aftereffects of substance abuse on both physical and mental thriving.

3.4 Rest Models

In the hustling around of current life, rest habitually takes an optional parlor. Nevertheless, its importance could never be more critical. Show up with us as we unwind the secrets of rest designs and their huge wellbeing impacts. From the periods of rest to the repercussions of absence of rest, this part gives huge pieces of information into creating sound rest affinities for all around flourishing.

4. Natural Components

4.1 Pollution and Toxins

Step into the area of natural prosperity as we examine the impact of defilement and toxins on our success. Find out about potential sources of natural poisons and how air, water, and soil quality can affect our health. This portion outfits you with data to investigate an evidently dirtied world and make choices that advance a superior environment for yourself and individuals later on.

4.2 Climate and Environment

The environment connects past pollution, including climate and atmospheric conditions that impact our prosperity. Plunge into the association between climate conditions and different prosperity results. From the impact of temperature cutoff points to the results of ecological change, this portion uncovers understanding into the interconnectedness of normal components and human thriving.

5. Contaminations

5.1 Bacterial Contaminations As we investigate the various manifestations of bacterial diseases that can affect human health, we enter the infinite universe of microorganisms. From ordinary illnesses to extra outrageous conditions, we'll examine the causes, incidental effects, and preventive measures related with bacterial defilements. Understanding these minute enemies is basic to keeping a flexible insusceptible system.

5.2 Viral Infections

Contaminations can release decimation on the human body. Oblige us in unraveling the intricacies of viral defilements, from the ordinary cold to extra difficult ailments. Find out how immunization can help prevent viral diseases by examining the mechanisms by which infections attack our cells and bypass our defenses.

5.3 Infectious Illnesses

Parasites, but much of the time disregarded, expect a basic part in human prosperity. In this section, we'll jump into the universe of parasitic sicknesses, examining how these animals can cause an extent of conditions. From skin illnesses to principal afflictions, gain pieces of information into the components that add to infectious pollutions and systems for balance and treatment.

6. Constant Tension

6.1 Mental Impact

Bounce into the mind boggling relationship between constant strain and its huge mental impact. Research the psychological signs of pressure, its consequences for feelings, comprehension, and emotional well-being in general. Learn about the complex relationship between persistent stressors and mental health, from elevated tension to mental health issues.

6.2 Physiological Effects

Stress doesn't simply impact the mind — it makes a long-lasting engraving on the body. We break down the physiological effects of constant pressure in this section. From the appearance of stress synthetic compounds with the impact on crucial organs, dive into the confusing parts through which stress can show truly. Understanding these effects is basic for embracing frameworks to direct and adjust to steady tension.

7. Problems with the Safe Framework

7.1 Immune System Diseases Enter the world of immune system diseases, in which the body's resistant framework betrays the body it was designed to protect. Examine the instruments essential invulnerable framework issues, from rheumatoid joint aggravation to lupus. Find out about the hardships that individuals with immune system conditions face and the most recent medicines and treatment choices.

7.2 Immunodeficiency Issues while certain individuals battle with immunodeficiency problems, others battle with an overactive resistant framework. Explore the realm of compromised invulnerable capability by comprehending the conditions that render the body immune to disease. From acquired disorders to primary immunodeficiency's, this section sheds light on the complexity of immunodeficiency and its effects on overall health.

8. Age-Related Factors

8.1 Pediatric Ailments

Kids experience unique prosperity challenges unquestionable from those of adults. Explore the location of pediatric disorders, from ordinary youth pollutions to inborn conditions. This portion gives a careful framework of prosperity considerations planned for the pediatric people, drawing in watchmen and parental figures with data to protect the flourishing of the more young age.

8.2 Hindrances to Great Maturing

Wellbeing As we progress in years, our wellbeing necessities change. Uncover the prosperity challenges that go with the developing framework, from continuous conditions to mental corruption. Investigate strategies for protecting essentialness and personal satisfaction in later life as you explore the intricacy of geriatric wellbeing. This part fills in as a helper for individuals entering the splendid years and those truly zeroing in on lifelong companions and family.

9. Working environment Related Sicknesses

Word related dangers The work environment can be a wellspring of both satisfaction and medical problems. Examine the scope of infections related with various occupations, from word related dangers to long stretch prosperity ideas. Find out about working environment wellbeing practices and deterrent estimates that add to a better and more secure workplace.

9.2 Physical and Mental Stress

Word-related dangers encompass mental and profound prosperity beyond actual dangers. Look at the impacts of delayed anxiety on emotional wellness because of word related stressors. Figure out how to keep a sound balance between serious and fun activities and manage pressure in the working environment.

10. Social Determinants of Prosperity

10.1 Monetary Status

Prosperity is complicatedly associated with social and financial components. In this portion, we explore the tremendous impact of monetary status on all around prosperity results. Learn how social and financial factors contribute to health inconsistencies, from admission to medical care to lifestyle choices. The reason for supporting for fair medical care arrangements is this information.

10.2 Induction to Clinical consideration

Permission to clinical consideration is a fundamental determinant of prosperity results. Examine the obstacles people might face in order to obtain high-quality medical care, such as geographical and financial constraints. The need of comprehensive medical services frameworks is stressed in this part, which dives into the meaning of medical care availability and the expected ramifications for general wellbeing.

11. Lamentable Neatness and Cleansing

11.1 Waterborne Ailments

Dive into the fundamental relationship between appalling neatness and waterborne diseases. Explore how debased water sources can incite a scope of infections, from gastrointestinal pollutions to extra serious waterborne diseases. This section loosens up the meaning of clean water and convincing disinfection practices in protecting general prosperity.

11.2 Individual Neatness Practices

Our regular penchants expect a basic part in thwarting the spread of disorders. In this part, we explore the impact of individual neatness practices on individual and neighborhood. From handwashing to real sanitization workplaces, gain pieces of information into the practices that structure the essential line of security against sicknesses and add to for the most part prosperity.

12. Awarenesses and Responsive characteristics

12.1 Biological Allergens

Step into the space of responsive qualities set off by the environment. Examine the different bunch of regular allergens, from residue to pet dander. Learn the mechanisms by which the immune system responds to these allergens and practical insights into managing natural sensitivities for improved personal satisfaction.

12.2 Food Awareness's

Food can be a wellspring of delight, but for curtain's motivations, it addresses a bet of excessively touchy reactions. Plunge into the complexities of food awareness's, exploring typical allergens and the safe responses that can provoke threatening reactions. This portion provides guidance on investigating dietary constraints and ensuring the success of individuals with food awareness's.

13. Genital and Conceptive Prosperity

13.1 Genuinely Conveyed Pollutions

Investigate the location of genuinely conveyed pollutions (STIs) and their impact on genital and regenerative prosperity. This part takes a gander at the a wide range of kinds of STIs, from how to forestall them to treat them. It additionally shows that it is so essential to be protected and get ordinary screenings to keep your sexual wellbeing great.

13.2 Obstetrical and Conceptive

Issues a large number of obstetrical and regenerative issues influence ladies' wellbeing. Explore issues going from ladylike prosperity to regenerative issues. This portion gives a comprehensive framework of components affecting women's prosperity and offers pieces of information into proactive measures for staying aware of gynecological and conceptive flourishing.

14. Weak wellbeing

14.1 Undernutrition

Weak wellbeing connects past glutting — it consolidates insufficient sustenance moreover. Research the impacts of deficient dietary admission and the impacts of undernutrition on wellbeing. From micronutrient needs to blocked improvement, this part uncovers understanding into the overall trial of undernutrition and techniques for watching out for it.

14.2 Over nutrition

In a period of flood, overnutrition has emerged as a basic prosperity concern. Explore the consequences of overflow calorie use, from weight to related afflictions. This part gives encounters into the convoluted factors adding to overnutrition and techniques for progressing changed and helpful dietary examples.

15. Endocrine Issues

15.1 Diabetes

Enter the space of endocrine issues with an accentuation on diabetes — a condition with clearing repercussions for prosperity. Examine the various types of diabetes, the factors that lead to them, and the significance of monitoring blood glucose levels. This part outfits peruses with data about lifestyle components and clinical intercessions for preventing and directing diabetes.

15.2 Problems of the Thyroid The thyroid organ is significant for directing digestion and by and large wellbeing. Jump into the complexities of thyroid issues, from hyperthyroidism to hypothyroidism. Get pieces of information into the secondary effects, causes, and the leading group of thyroid conditions, empowering individuals to investigate the nuances of endocrine prosperity.

16. Cardiovascular

Parts 16.1 Heart Ailments The heart is the point of convergence of cardiovascular prosperity, and heart contaminations present serious prosperity bets. Look at the different sorts of heart conditions, from coronary vein infection to cardiovascular breakdown. Risk factors, shield measures, and way of life decisions that add to heart flourishing are examined beginning to end in this part.

16.2 Hypertension

Hypertension, or hypertension, is a key cardiovascular part with all over prospering considerations. Reveal the complexities of hypertension, investigating its impact on heart thriving and for the most part around prospering. Learn about assurance measures and lifestyle changes that have a few command over circulatory strain and lower the bet of cardiovascular events.

17. Respiratory Issues

17.1 Asthma

Investigate the whimsical universe of asthma, a consistent respiratory condition that impacts millions from one side of the world to the other. Research the triggers, discretionary effects, and the supervisors approaches for asthma. This part gives typical scraps of information into staying aware of respiratory thriving and restricting the impact of asthma on normal presence.

17.2 Constant Obstructive Pneumonic Tainting (COPD) COPD is described by persevering bronchitis and emphysema as well as other moderate respiratory issues. Learn about the intricacies of COPD, its causes, and the significance of early intervention by diving into its intricacies. This segment gives clients data with respect to way of life changes and clinical proposals for COPD management.

18. Issues with the Sensory system

18.1 Alzheimer's Illness Alzheimer's sickness, a kind of dementia, presents novel deterrents to neurological wellbeing. Research the complexities of Alzheimer's infection, including its starting points and potential gamble factors. This part uncovers understanding into the significance of mental achievement and offers pieces of information into procedures for pushing frontal cortex flourishing and organizing the impact of Alzheimer's.

18.2 Parkinson's Disorder

Enter the space of Parkinson's disorder, an excellent neurological issue affecting improvement. Reveal Parkinson's delayed effects, causes, and pioneering treatments. This part gives tremendous encounters into staying aware of individual fulfillment for individuals affected by Parkinson's and those related with their thought.

19. Stomach related System Issues

19.1 Gastrointestinal Defilements

The stomach related system can go against various troubles, including defilements that impact gastrointestinal flourishing. Learn about the symptoms, effects, and treatments for gastrointestinal conditions. This part gives per users the information they hope to go with taught choices concerning how to stay aware of their stomach related prosperity and thwart infection spread.

19.2 Provocative Inside Infirmities

Complex inconveniences to stomach related success are introduced by flammable entrails messes (IBD), like Crohn's illness and ulcerative colitis. Plunge into the intricacies of IBD, investigating the discretionary effects, causes, and the managers frameworks. People researching the intricacies of burning intestine difficulties can benefit from the experiences provided in this section.

20. Hormonal unpredictability

20.1 Conceptive Synthetics It is anticipated that the delicate equilibrium of conceptive synthetics will play a significant role overall. Examine the effects of hormonal imbalances on regenerative prosperity, including issues with readiness and female irregularities. Methods for remaining mindful of hormonal equilibrium and snippets of data into the parts that impact conceptive artificial materials are given in this segment.

20.2 Issues of the Improvement Engineered intensifies Issues of the headway fabricated materials can influence individuals, taking everything into account, influencing their certified new turn of events and generally thriving. Find the complexities of compound improvement issues by reviewing their causes, logical medications, and optional impacts. This part gives enormous pieces of information to individuals investigating the troubles related with progress compound uncommon nature.

21. Dental and Oral Wellbeing

21.1 Holes and Gum Illness Bring a profound jump into the subject of dental and oral wellbeing by finding out about the normal issues brought about by gum infection and dejections. Sort out the causes, preventive measures, and treatment decisions for staying aware of ideal oral tidiness. This part gives parsers functional data for forestalling and settling general dental issues.

21.2 Oral Tumors Oral developments impact various bits of the mouth and throat and address a serious risk to prosperity. Research the bet factors, unintentional effects, and preventive measures for oral illnesses. This section discusses the significance of early area and comprehensive oral health practices in reducing the impact of oral diseases.

22. Acute or chronic traumatic wounds

resulting from falls and other accidents Learn about the various types of wounds that can occur, such as head injuries and breaks. This segment talks about safeguard measures and clinical guide frameworks for treating serious injuries.

22.2 Games Wounds

Partaking in sports goes with its piece of injury bets. Research the degree of sports wounds, from wounds to power outages. This part offers reasonable bearing on injury presumption, authentic sports gear, and procedures for coordinating and recovering from sports-related injuries.

23. Diseases of the System

23.1 Rheumatoid Joint Problem Rheumatoid joint problem is a disease of the System that affects the joints and causes pain and fuel. Uncover the complexities of rheumatoid joint torment, investigating its impact on joint achievement and in standard flourishing. This part gives bits of information into treatment decisions and lifestyle changes for planning rheumatoid joint compounding.

23.2 Lupus An essential safe system disorder that can influence different organs and tissues, lupus can influence the whole body. Examine the baffling concept of lupus, its delayed effects, causes, and potential complications. This segment furnishes lupus victims and their guardians with the data they need to more readily deal with the condition and work toward individual satisfaction.

24. Tainting

24.1 Gained Factors

Take a gander at the control of genetic components in subverting improvement development. Learn how acquired tendencies can accumulate weakness to express various diseases. For people who have a family groundwork of sickness, this part examines the significance of acquired testing, early affirmation, and safety efforts.

24.2 Standard Causes

Standard parts can all around add to defilement risk. Jump into the impact of environmental causes, similar to receptiveness to undermining advancement causing prepared experts and contaminations, on affliction improvement. This part gives experiences into lessening environment related dangers and pursuing way of life decisions that guide in forestalling disease development.

25. Hostile Medicine Reactions

Although medications play an important role in the treatment of a variety of conditions, they can also have negative effects. Examine the degree of compromising prescription reactions, from delicate to mind blowing. This piece provides guidance on seeing and administering medication conceded results, focusing in on the significance of open correspondence with clinical benefits providers.

25.2 Polypharmacy The usage of different solutions, or polypharmacy, can be extraordinarily horrendous to one's prosperity. Think about the advantages and disadvantages of taking multiple medications as you learn about the intricacies of polypharmacy. In this section, which provides concrete information on solution organization, the significance of coordination among clinical consideration providers to work on supportive outcomes is emphasized.

26. Psychological Factors

26.1 Mental Health Disorders

Examine conditions like bipolar disorder, depression, and anxiety to learn more about the complex world of mental health disorders. Figure out the effect of mental elements on mental prosperity and gain bits of knowledge into the significance of early intercession, treatment choices, and destigmatizing emotional well-being difficulties.

26.2 Pressure Related Diseases

Mental pressure can appear in different actual sicknesses. Investigate the different exhibit of pressure related ailments, from cardiovascular issues to stomach related issues. This part gives functional methodologies to push the board and cultivating mental strength for generally wellbeing.

27. Rest Problems

27.1 Sleep deprivation

Rest is fundamental for generally prosperity, however a sleeping disorder can upset this urgent part of wellbeing. Investigate both short-term and long-term sleep disturbances to learn more about the causes and effects of insomnia. This segment gives experiences into rest cleanliness rehearses and social intercessions for further developing rest quality.

27.2 Sleep Apnea During sleep, sleep apnea presents unique challenges to cardiovascular and respiratory health. Explore the various types, symptoms, and potential health effects of sleep apnea to learn more about its intricacies. This part gives direction on indicative techniques and treatment choices for overseeing rest apnea and further developing rest related wellbeing.

28. Nutritional Deficiencies

28.1 Vitamin Deficiencies Investigate the effects of vitamin deficiency on health, including problems with the nervous system and immune system. Dig into the wellsprings of fundamental nutrients and gain experiences into forestalling and tending to lacks through a decent and supplement rich eating routine.

28.2 Mineral Deficiencies Mineral deficiencies can cause health problems because minerals are necessary for a variety of physiological processes. Uncover the outcomes of lacks of mineral, from bone wellbeing to energy digestion. This part gives functional direction on keeping up with ideal mineral levels through dietary decisions and supplementation when important.

29. Drying out

29.1 Effect on Wellbeing

Comprehend the basic job of hydration in keeping up with in general wellbeing. Investigate the effect of parchedness on different physical processes, from mental execution to kidney capability. This segment underscores the significance of sufficient liquid admission for ideal wellbeing and gives bits of knowledge into perceiving and forestalling parchedness.

29.2 Signs and Symptoms It is essential for prompt intervention to recognize the signs and symptoms of dehydration. Dig into the appearances of lack of hydration, from ache to tipsiness. This segment outfits parsers with information to distinguish parchedness and offers reasonable ways to remain enough hydrated.

30. Dietary Propensities

30.1 Unfortunate Eating Examples

Investigate the results of unfortunate eating designs on physical and mental prosperity.

From unfortunate nourishment to profound eating, comprehend what dietary propensities mean for wellbeing results. This part gives experiences into developing careful eating pursues and taking on routines that help in general wellbeing.

30.2 Effect on Digestion

Dietary propensities assume a critical part in digestion, impacting energy equilibrium and weight the board. Dive into the association between dietary decisions and metabolic wellbeing. This segment gives reasonable direction on encouraging a digestion strong eating regimen and way of life for long haul prosperity.

31. Lacking Real work

31.1 Inactive Way of life

Research the repercussions of a dormant way of life on in ordinary thriving. Research the effects of long inactivity, including cardiovascular risks and external muscle issues. This section provides straightforward advice on the best way to incorporate development into daily life for improved mental and physical health.

31.2 Activity and Flourishing

Handle the pleasant relationship among exercise and flourishing. Look at the different advantages of standard actual work, from mental prosperity to cardiovascular wellbeing. This part offers counsel on the most effective way to make an action arrangement that is modified to each individual's necessities and stimulates a lifestyle of standard genuine work.

32. Addictions

32.1 Substance Enslavement

Enslavement can generally impact physical and up close and personal thriving. To get more familiar with substance dependence's intricacy, explore its neurobiological establishments and hardships in recuperation. This part gives experiences into avoidance, mediation, and steady systems for people affected by substance misuse.

32.2 Social Addictions

Past substances, affinity outlining ways to deal with acting can appear in different bits of life. Look at social addictions, from gaming to steady shopping. This section provides guidance on empowering healthy tendencies and strategies for managing particularly challenging times, as well as insight into the psychological aspects of social addiction.

33.Ramifications for Mental and Genuine

Strength of Social Separation Social confinement can generally influence mental and real prosperity. Inspect the connections that exist among dejection and conditions like sadness and cardiovascular sickness. This section emphasizes the significance of social connections for one's overall wellbeing and discusses strategies for combating social isolation.

33.2 Infection and Wretchedness

Check out at the relationship among affliction and hopelessness by sorting out how social isolation can escalate an arrangement of clinical issues. As a preventative measure against the terrible effects of sadness, this section provides information on building and maintaining large social relationships.

34. Nonappearance of Vaccination

34.1 Significance of Vaccination

Perceive the major job that immunization plays in forestalling the spread of irresistible illnesses. Analyze the advantages of inoculation for people and organizations. This section gives data on the importance of fortunate immunizations in remaining mindful of general flourishing.

34.2 Preventable Disorders Investigate the occupation of vaccinations in the evasion of preventable diseases. This part tends to normal worries and ambiguities encompassing inoculations and gives knowledge into explicit sicknesses that can be mitigated through immunization, from juvenile vaccinations to grown-up supports.

35. Family Orchestrating:

Regenerative Choices Conceptive choices basically influence family orchestrating and individual thriving. Explore the various highlights of family orchestrating, including readiness care and strategies for contraception. This part gives data on settling on informed conceptive decisions in course of action with individual objectives.

35.2 Issues Connecting with Pregnancy Study the intricacies of pregnancy and origination. From pre-birth care to post pregnancy challenges, this part watches out for a degree of issues related with pregnancy. Gather information regarding ideal conceptual prosperity and the various phases of the regenerative excursion.

36. Acceptance of Radiations

36.1 Ionizing Radiation Recognize the potential threats to one's health posed by ionizing radiation, which can come from industrial or environmental sources. This part looks at the standards of radiation straightforwardness and offers seminar on confining dangers and remaining mindful of radiation security.

36.2 Non-Ionizing Radiation Investigate the field of non-ionizing radiation, including its sources, which include electromagnetic fields and radiofrequency waves. By delving into the logical understanding of non-ionizing radiation, you can learn practical strategies for reducing openness and improving well-being.

37. Lack of Access to Clinical Consideration

37.1 Preventative Measures for Clinical Consideration Inadequate access to clinical consideration can result in fundamental obstacles to success. Look at the deterrents that individuals could experience, like monetary necessities or geological requirements. This part watches out for the significance of addressing clinical thought anomalies and raising fair authorization to clinical benefits.

37.2 In general Assortments

In general clinical advantages aberrations add to combinations in success results all around the planet. Jump into the parts adding to these assortments and look at expected manages any results with respect to accomplishing generally speaking success regard. This part underlines the importance of accommodating endeavors in watching out for clinical advantages access on a general scale.

38. Misuse of Drugs:

Maladaptive ways of managing pressure or difficulty Maladaptive ways of managing pressure or difficulty, such as utilizing drugs, can hurt your psychological and actual wellbeing. Research the relationship between sad strategy for practical adaptations and stress. This section sheds light on the differences between adopting more adaptable strategies for coping with life's challenges and maladaptive ways of acting.

38.2 Avoidant Behavior Despite substance abuse, avoidant behavior can make it harder to truly adapt. Consider the effects of aversion on mental health and strategies for overcoming evasion tendencies. This piece centers around the importance of making versatile ways to deal with overseeing especially problematic times for strength and thriving.

39. Red hot Conditions

39.1 Steady Bothering Determined disturbance is connected to various illnesses, including cardiovascular issues and safe framework problems. Examine the causes and effects of constant stress for insight into lifestyle choices that can reduce stress and increase overall prosperity.

39.2 Effect on Organs

Plunge into the particular organs impacted by flammable circumstances, understanding how enterprising worsening can add to organ harm and brokenness. This part gives down to earth direction on taking on calming tendencies and diminishing the bet of provocative related thriving difficulties.

40. Sad Dental Neatness

40.1 Oral Thriving and In regular Achievement

Figure out the fundamental connection between oral thriving and generally achievement. Research the effects of appalling oral tidiness on the body all things considered, integrating issues with the heart and the lungs. This section gives up experiences into saving with ideal oral flourishing for a predominant life.

40.2 Gum Infections and Focal Success

Gum infections can have clearing impacts past oral success. Hop into the relationship between gum issues and essential ailments, including diabetes and cardiovascular illnesses. This part offers utilitarian approaches to forestalling gum diseases and remaining mindful of gum success for in ordinary thriving.

41. Autoinflammatory Sicknesses

41.1 Frameworks of Autoinflammation

Examine the baffling parts essential autoinflammatory ailments. From dysregulation of the safe structure to genetic components, this part jumps into the explanations behind autoinflammation and the extraordinary hardships it presents in the area of resistant framework issues.

41.2 Instances of Autoinflammatory Illnesses Find out about unambiguous autoinflammatory sicknesses like Behçet's infection and familial Mediterranean Fever (FMF). Handle the characteristics, incidental effects, and the board procedures for these conditions, uncovering understanding into the different scope of autoinflammatory diseases.

42. 42.1 Effect on General Wellbeing

Lacking disinfection can possibly essentially affect general wellbeing. Research the repercussions of lamentable disinfection practices on networks, from the spread of overpowering diseases to compromised water quality. This part emphasizes the meaning of cleansing establishment in progressing commonly broad prosperity.

42.2 Waterborne Diseases

Concentrate on the specific health risks posed by insufficient sanitation, particularly waterborne diseases. Figure out how cholera and diarrhea episodes can be welcomed on by sullied water sources. This section discusses preventative measures and the fundamental role disinfection plays in ensuring access to clean water.

43. Excessive Screen Time

43.1 Mechanized Eye Strain

Superfluous screen time has become overwhelming in the automated age, influencing eye prosperity. Research the characteristic of cutting edge eye strain and its incidental effects. This fragment offers realistic ways of decreasing eye strain and staying aware of visual thriving in the time of undeniable high level advancement.

43.2 Impact on Profound health

Past genuine effects, unreasonable screen time can affect close to home prosperity. Plunge into the psychological impact of long screen receptiveness, from extended sensations of nervousness to disturb rest plans. This part provides guidance on spreading out strong screen time inclinations for chipped away at mental flourishing.

44. Organ Frustrations

44.1 Kidney Frustration

Kidney frustration is a serious clinical issue with complex consequences. Explore the causes, incidental effects, and the leading group of kidney disillusionment. This part gives pieces of information into preventive measures and lifestyle choices that help kidney prosperity.

44.2 Liver Disappointment Liver disappointment is exceptionally terrible for your wellbeing all in all. Find out about liver disappointment's circumstances and end results, as well as the meaning of liver capability for different physiological cycles. This part offers useful heading on staying aware of liver prosperity and thwarting liver-related issues.

45. Lack of Sun Protection

45.1 Skin Malignant Growth Lack of sun protection can improve skin disease. Examine the various types of skin diseases, risk factors, and treatment options. This fragment focuses on the meaning of sun prosperity practices in decreasing the bet of skin harmful development.

45.2 Sun related consume and Long stretch Effects

Dive into the speedy and long stretch effects of sun related consume, understanding how preposterous sun receptiveness can incite skin hurt and troublesome developing. This part gives conventional tips to convincing sun protection and restricting the bet of consume from the sun related challenges.

46. Creature Related Contaminations

46.1 Zoonotic Illnesses Spotlight on zoonotic sicknesses to examine the potential wellbeing gambles with presented by creature contact. Grasp how compelling experts can be imparted from animals to individuals and gain pieces of information into preventive measures. This section emphasizes responsible pet ownership and secure interactions with animals.

46.2 Pet-Related Sicknesses

Hop into express illnesses that can be imparted from pets to individuals. From ringworm to leptospirosis, grasp the risks and preventive measures related with pet-related defilements. This fragment provides guidance on empowering a sound bond with pets while restricting prosperity possibilities.

47. Unreasonable Clamor Openness

47.1 Hearing Misfortune
Unreasonable clamor openness can lead to hearing misfortune, a common but avoidable health issue. Research the parts of upheaval induced hearing mischief and gain pieces of information into safeguarding efforts. This section emphasizes the significance of

hearing conservation for maintaining auditory health.

47.2 Cardiovascular Impact

Past hearing mishap, superfluous fuss transparency can have cardiovascular repercussions. Examine the association between heart wellbeing and commotion contamination by figuring out how stressors connected with clamor can intensify heart issues. This part gives practical systems to restricting over the top upheaval transparency for cardiovascular flourishing.

48. 48.1 Explore the causes, risks, and the leading body of gestational diabetes. This section gives encounters into propelling a strong pregnancy and reducing the bet of

gestational diabetes-related burdens.

48.2 Blood poisoning

Blood poisoning is a serious pregnancy-related condition that warrants thought. This part offers heading on noticing and managing blood poisoning takes a risk for dealt with maternal and fetal prosperity.

49. 49.1 Medication actuated Autoimmunity

Find out about the confounded peculiarity of medication incited autoimmunity and how certain prescriptions can cause immune system responses. Plunge into examples of meds related with safe framework responses and gain pieces of information into the organization and expectation of drug affected autoimmunity.

49.2 Administration and Counteraction Investigate ways of controlling immune system responses to meds, such as changing treatment plans or halting medications that aren't working. This section provides judicious guidance to clinical consideration providers and patients in investigating the complexities of prescription impelled autoimmunity.

50. End

50.1 Recap of Focal issues

Summarize the focal issues analyzed all through the helper, highlighting the interconnected thought of various factors that add to infirmity. This decision section serves as a comprehensive summary of the aid's previous knowledge, promoting a comprehensive understanding of prosperity and well-being.

[Note: The perfection was abbreviated. Feel free to inquire if you have explicit requests for the conclusion or additional segments.]